Bush Baby
Coloring Book
For Adults

30 Hand Drawn Paisley and Henna
Folk Art Style Gagalo Coloring Pages

By
Louise Ford

Copyright © 2016
All rights Reserved.

ISBN-13: 978-1541071087
ISBN-10: 1541071085

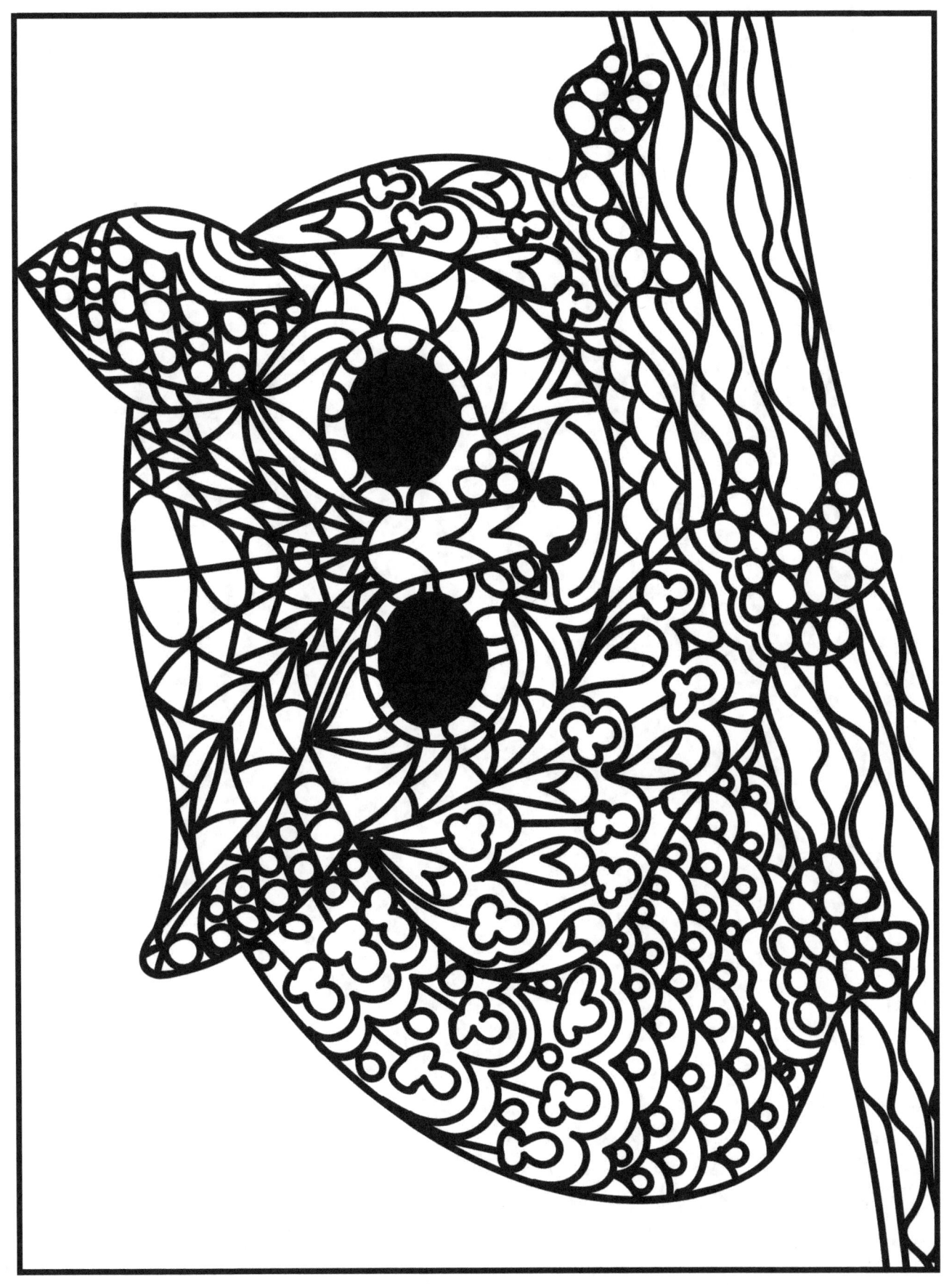

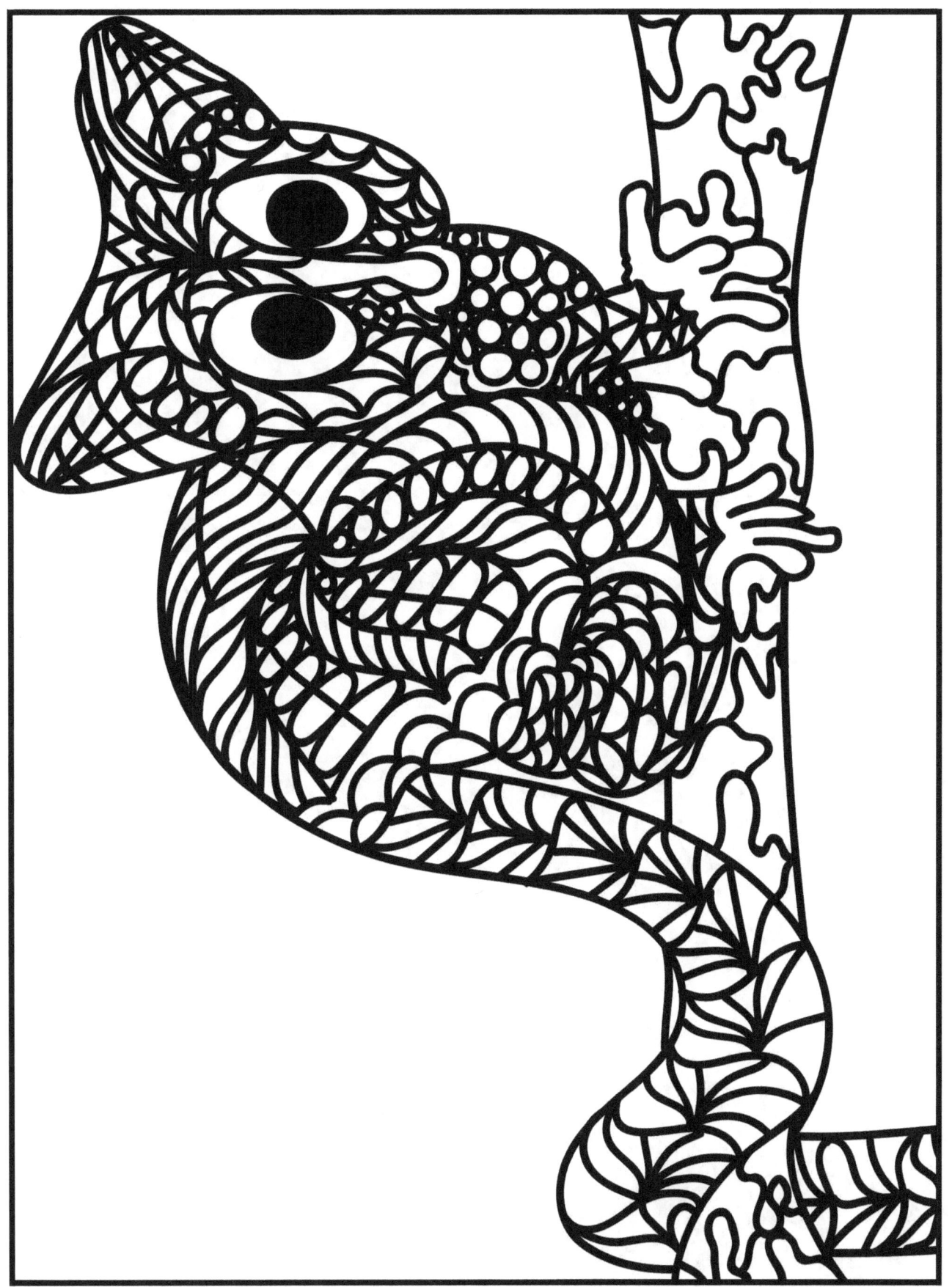

www.ingramcontent.com/pod-product-compliance
Lightning Source LLC
Chambersburg PA
CBHW081859280526
45789CB00007B/2759